SUMMER PATTERNS, PROJECTS & PLANS

by
Imogene Forte

Incentive Publications, Inc.
Nashville, Tennessee

Illustrated by Gayle Seaberg Harvey
Cover by Susan Eaddy
Edited by Dianna Richey

ISBN 0-86530-218-9

Table Of Contents

PREFACE

Summer – June, July, and August, too!

SUMMER ...

... A TIME of special days and warm weather activities – taking nature walks; planning and completing indoor and outdoor projects; getting to know the community; and enjoying plays, parties, and parades with friends.

... A TIME of celebrating the summer season – sharing books and ideas in a relaxed setting, learning outdoor safety rules, and creating a treasury of memories and lessons in the Super Summer Journal to keep throughout the year.

All of this and more is the excitement of June, July, and August waiting to be brought into your "come alive" classroom. Watch students' eyes brighten as your classroom says, "Summer is here!" from the ceiling to the floor, from windows and doors, from work sheets and activity projects, from stories and books, and especially from you – an enthusiastic, "project planned" teacher.

This little book of SUMMER PATTERNS, PROJECTS & PLANS has been put together with tender loving care to help you be prepared to meet every one of the summer days in June, July, and August with special treats, learning projects, and fun surprises that will make your students eager to participate in every phase of the daily schedule and look forward to the next day. Best of all, the patterns, projects, and plans are ready for quick and easy use and require no elaborate materials and very little advance preparation.

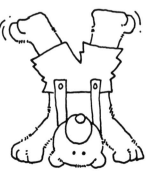

For your convenience, the materials in this book have been organized around four major unit themes. Each of the patterns, projects, and plans can be used independently of the unit plan. However, to be just as effective in classrooms in which teachers choose not to use a unit approach, all are planned to complement and enrich adopted curriculum schemes and to meet young children's interests and learning needs.

Major unit themes include:
- Suddenly Summer
- June Joy
- Jolly July
- Ten Terrific Things To Do In August

Each unit includes a major objective and things to do; poster/booklet cover, bulletin board, or display; patterns; art and/or an assembly project; reproducible basic skills activities; and book, story, and poem suggestions to make the literature connection.

Other topics, special days, and events for which patterns, projects, and plans have been provided include:

- Outdoor Safety
- Self-Awareness
- Hip, Hip Hooray! A Parade is on the Way!

SUDDENLY SUMMER

Major Objective:
Children will develop awareness of the colors, sights, sounds, and special events that characterize the months of June, July, and August.

Things To Do:
- Use the patterns in this book to make decorations for doors, windows, desks, wall borders, chalkboard borders, etc.

- Create "Signs of Summer" mobiles. Ask the children to draw their favorite symbol of summer (birds, flowers, sun, water, or outdoor activities, etc.) Or, have them color favorite summer patterns from pages 25, 33, 34, 49, and 72. Attach the completed artwork to various lengths of yarn and tie yarn to clothes hangers to create "Signs of Summer" mobiles.

- Design your own Monthly Classroom Management Chart by pasting the appropriate heading and art (page 13) to represent each month to the blank chart (page 12).

- Introduce the Super Summer Journal (pages 15 - 19) by telling students a special time will be set aside each month to record summer memories. Discuss with them why people want to save memories. Explain that a journal records the special happenings and how a person feels about the events. The Super Summer Journal will be their own personal record of this summer. Introduce the reproducible pages for each month; save the completed pages until the end of the session. At the end of the summer, assist children in completing the journal cover. (You may also include any of the activities in this book, photos, artwork, or other appropriate materials.) Staple (or hole-punch and tie with yarn) the pages together to make a take-home booklet to provide a lasting memory of their special summer.

To complete the activities in this book, you will need:

crayons & markers	cotton balls	paper towels
construction paper	glitter	crepe paper
tape	straight pins	streamer
paste	foil	wire clothes hangers
scissors	gift wrap	tissue paper
stapler	yarn	dowel sticks
pencils	tagboard	
drawing paper	paper cups	
tempera paint	ingredients for recipes (pages 29 and 61)	

Dear Parents,

Summer is here, and that means our classroom is all set for lots of warm weather learning and fun in the sun.

It is time to celebrate the arrival of the summer season. We are excited about taking nature walks; getting to know the community; learning outdoor safety rules; and enjoying plays, parties, and parades with friends.

During the days and weeks ahead, we will be cutting and pasting, experimenting and exploring, creating and discovering, and learning many new and exciting things to share in a relaxed setting.

Your child will bring home artwork, recipes, stories, papers, and other special projects to share with you. Your encouragement and reinforcement will boost your child's self-esteem as well as help to stimulate future creative development and the desire to learn.

You may help with our monthly projects by collecting and contributing paper sacks, good "act out" books, stories, rhymes, scrap copy paper, yarn, buttons, and other miscellaneous art materials. Anything you would like to contribute or do to enhance our summer celebration would be greatly appreciated.

Sincerely,

SUMMER ALPHABET

A ... All about summer fun
B ... Butterflies, bees, and birds
C ... Castles in the clouds
D ... Days are getting longer!
E ... Everywhere, everywhere, summer's here!
F ... Fresh air, sunshine, and exercise
G ... Growing green gardens
H ... Hot dogs, hamburgers on the grill
I ... Ice cream, Popsicles®, and soda pop
J ... June, July, and August, too!
K ... Kites flying high in the sky
L ... Lemonade to drink in the shade
M ... Many hours to play
N ... New games, new songs, and new books
O ... Out to play!
P ... Picnics, parties, and parades
Q ... Quilts for a picnic
R ... Ready to learn something new
S ... Sudden summer showers
T ... Trees to climb
U ... Under the shining sun
V ... Vacation getaway!
W ... Warm days to while away
X ... X-ploring nature's treasures
Y ... You're special!
Z ... ZZZZZ, time to nap

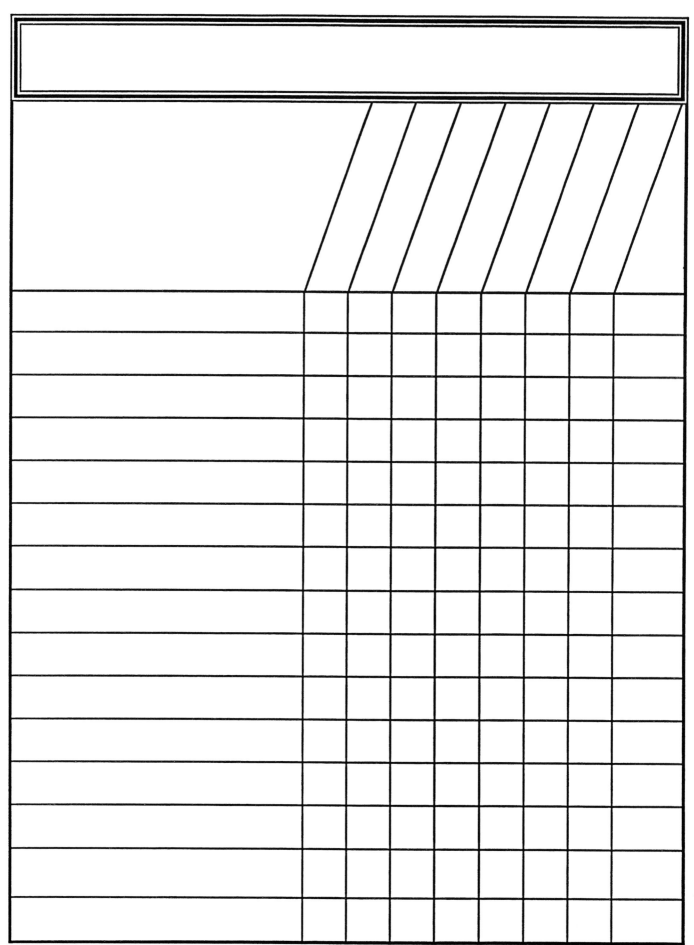

MANAGEMENT CHART HEADINGS

SUMMER MANAGEMENT CHART

JUNE MANAGEMENT CHART

JULY MANAGEMENT CHART

AUGUST MANAGEMENT CHART

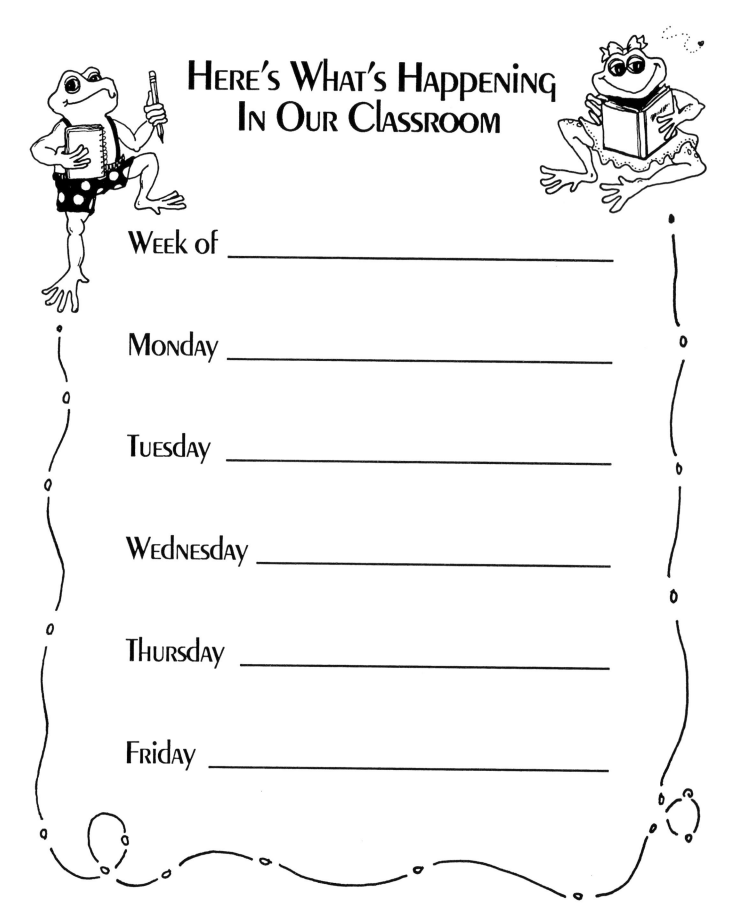

HERE'S WHAT'S HAPPENING IN OUR CLASSROOM

Week of _____

Monday _____

Tuesday _____

Wednesday _____

Thursday _____

Friday _____

My Super Summer Journal

Name _____

Date _____

Here I Am

My name is _____

I am _____ years old.

This is how I look.

JUNE

SOUNDS

SIGHTS

EVENTS

Name _____

Date _____

July

Sights

Sounds

Events

Name _____

Date _____

AUGUST

SIGHTS

SOUNDS

EVENTS

Name _____

Date _____

SUMMER BULLETIN BOARD BORDERS

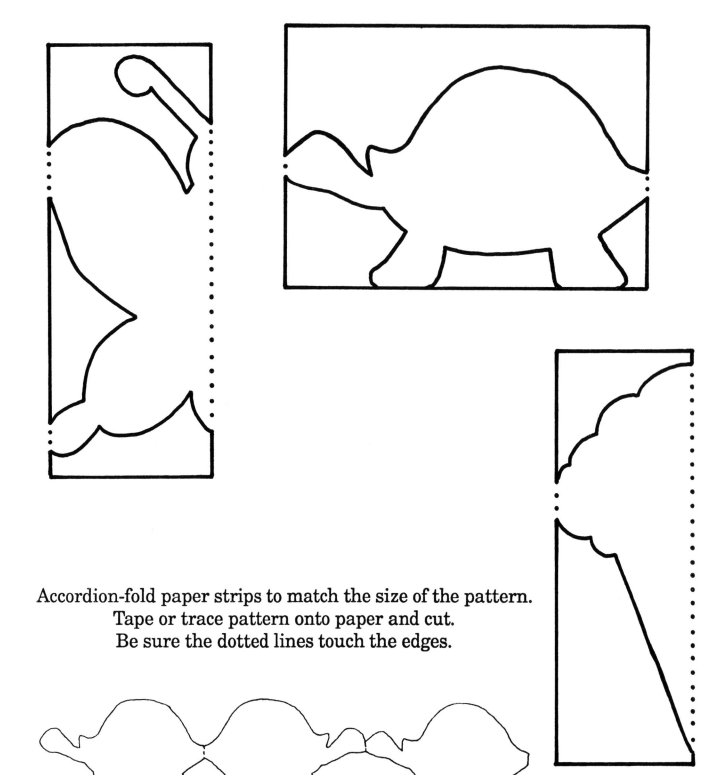

Accordion-fold paper strips to match the size of the pattern.
Tape or trace pattern onto paper and cut.
Be sure the dotted lines touch the edges.

WAYS TO USE THE SUMMER BULLETIN BOARD BORDERS

SUNSHINE SHOW-OFF

To "show off" good work, help children color and cut out sunshine show-offs. Show-offs make excellent "take-homes" or can be added to the Super Summer Journal pages.

Attach paper here.

SUMMER IS HERE

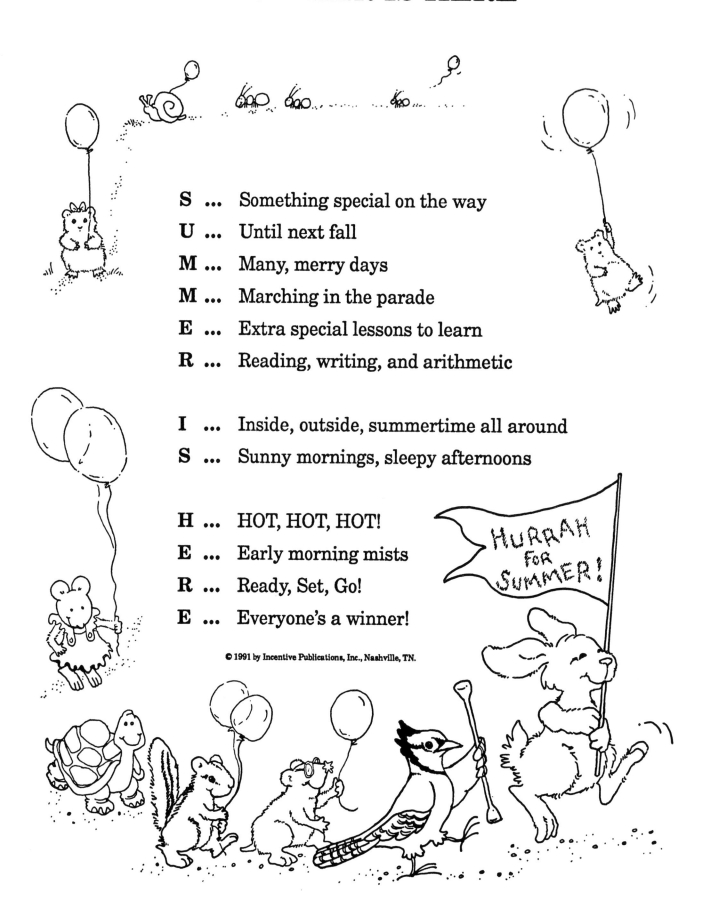

S ... Something special on the way

U ... Until next fall

M ... Many, merry days

M ... Marching in the parade

E ... Extra special lessons to learn

R ... Reading, writing, and arithmetic

I ... Inside, outside, summertime all around

S ... Sunny mornings, sleepy afternoons

H ... HOT, HOT, HOT!

E ... Early morning mists

R ... Ready, Set, Go!

E ... Everyone's a winner!

HURRAH FOR SUMMER!

SUPER SUMMER

SUMMER IS HERE,
GIVE A CHEER!

THINGS TO DO WITH SUMMER IS HERE POSTER

- Use the poster for a booklet cover. Have each child draw or paint a summer scene. Staple the finished pictures to the cover to make a picture book for the reading table. At the end of the summer, you can add the drawings to each child's Super Summer Journal (pages 15 - 19). Be sure to have each child write his/her name on his/her artwork.

- Reproduce the poster for each child to take home to color and discuss with the family as a "happy homework" assignment.

- Enlarge the poster and use as a discussion starter or a creative story motivator.

- Reproduce the poster for each child and use as a directed activity to reinforce listening and following directions skills. Adjust the time expectancies and number of directions according to the children's readiness level:

1. Color 4 birds.
2. Circle 2 birds' nests.
3. Draw 5 eggs in the empty nest.
4. Color the birdhouse blue.
5. Draw a sun in the sky.
6. Color the sun yellow.
7. Circle the rabbit.
8. Color 3 flowers.
9. Circle the butterfly near the rose.
10. Color the butterfly above the daisy.
11. Color the sky blue and the grass green.
12. Draw another child in the picture.
13. Give each of the children a name.
14. Make up a story about the children.
15. Give the picture another name.

PENCIL TOPPERS

Top your pencils with a summer blossom!
Color and cut out the pencil toppers below.

JUNE JOY

Major Objective:
Children will develop awareness of and appreciation for colors, sights, sounds, and seasonal changes that characterize June.

Things To Do:

- Take the class on a "Feeling Walk." Ask them to touch grass, sand, a running stream, pavement, concrete, stones, tree bark, and flower petals. Ask them to supply words to describe how each object feels. You may want to make a chart with appropriate vocabulary words before the walk.
Example: rough, silky, smooth, cool, slimy, gritty, etc.

- June is a perfect month to surprise the class with a special "field trip" to the playground. Ask them to sit or lie on the ground and "read the clouds." Children will enjoy using their imagination to create different pictures in the sky. Back in the classroom, have children draw their "cloud pictures." (Use cotton balls for a three-dimensional effect.)

- Have a Pasting Party. Take the class on a nature hunt. Help each child collect an odd-shaped stick or stone. Back in the classroom, make funny characters or animals with the objects by pasting buttons, pipe cleaners, construction paper, etc., to the sticks and stones.

- Children will love eating "dirt" that tastes great. In a large bowl, mix a quart tub of whipped topping, one package chocolate pudding mix, 1/2 cup milk, and 1 cup crushed Oreo® cookies. Blend until creamy. Pour into a foil-lined, clay flowerpot. Top mixture with another cup of crushed cookies. Add fake flowers. After lunch, serve the "dirt" in paper cups with plastic spoons. Enjoy!

A SILLY SUMMER SHOWER

Color everything in the picture except the mistakes.
Make an "X" on 7 funny, mixed-up mistakes.

Visual closure/finding mistakes

SWINGING INTO SUMMER FUN

Construction:

1. Enlarge the patterns on pages 33 and 34 and cut them out of colored construction paper.
2. Cut letters for the caption "Swinging Into Summer Fun" out of construction paper.
3. Have children draw and cut out additional birds, butterflies, flowers, etc., to add to the display. (Optional.)
4. Have children draw pictures of themselves involved in summer fun activities to add to the board.
5. Paste or tape each drawing on construction paper to create a bright border.
6. Assemble the board as shown above.

Variation: Substitute any one of the following captions. Ask children to draw appropriate pictures or symbols to be added to the board.

- "Swinging Into Summer With Good Books"
- "Swinging Into Summer With Good Work Habits"
- "Swinging Into Summer With Good Health Habits"
- "Swinging Into Summer With Good Manners"

SUMMER FUN PATTERNS

SUMMER FUN PATTERNS

AWARDS

JUNE DOORKNOB DECORATION

Color and cut out this doorknob decoration.
Hang it on your door to say that summer is here.

JOLLY JULY

Major Objective:
Children will develop an understanding of themselves and others and the interdependence of people who work and play together.

Things To Do:

- Friendly, funny, furious faces. Have one child "act out" an emotion using only his/her face. The rest of the class must guess what he or she is feeling and present a response to the emotion. Take turns until all children have had an opportunity to present a "face."

- Reproduce the coat of arms pattern (page 57) for each child to take home. Instruct children to ask family members to help complete coat of arms to represent their family heritage. Provide show-and tell-time for sharing completed coats of arms.

- Begin with a bag and end with a costume. Ask children to bring paper grocery sacks from home. Help each child create a costume by drawing and pasting elements to the bag. After the "costume" is completed, slit a hole in the top of the sack (large enough for child to push his/her head through without ripping the paper). Cut circles on either side of the bag for little arms. You can use the bag costumes for the Costume Party Parade on page 52.

- Sun and shadows. On a sunny day, take the class outside. Divide the children into pairs. Give each pair two large sheets of drawing paper. Help tape paper to the side of the building. (Make sure the sun is behind you so a shadow will be cast on the paper.) Position one child so that his/her silhouette shadow appears on the paper. Have the partner trace the shadow. After one "drawing" is complete, switch partners to allow the other a turn to be "drawn." This activity makes a great addition to the Super Summer Journal pages.

COME TO THE CIRCUS

Construction:

1. Enlarge the animal patterns on pages 39 - 45 and color them with markers or cut them out of colored construction paper.
2. Cut letters for the caption "Come To The Circus" out of construction paper or print it on a paper banner or sentence strip.
3. Assemble the board as shown above.

Use:

1. Place books about the circus on a table near the board for fun reading.
2. Have children act out various circus roles. (Look in books or magazines for other ideas for children to act out.)
3. Plan a circus day, complete with a parade, of course. Don't forget the popcorn and peanuts!

CIRCUS CLOWN

ELEPHANT

DRUMMER

MONKEYS & SEAL

LION & LION TAMER

BEAR

RINGMASTER

PACK A PICNIC BASKET

Cut and paste 5 foods in the basket to show a healthy picnic lunch.

Making food choices

Name _____

A SUMMER PICNIC

The animals are on their way to a summer picnic.
Trace a path to help each animal get to the picnic on time.

Visual discrimination

COOL TREATS FOR HOT DAYS

COOL TREATS BORDERS

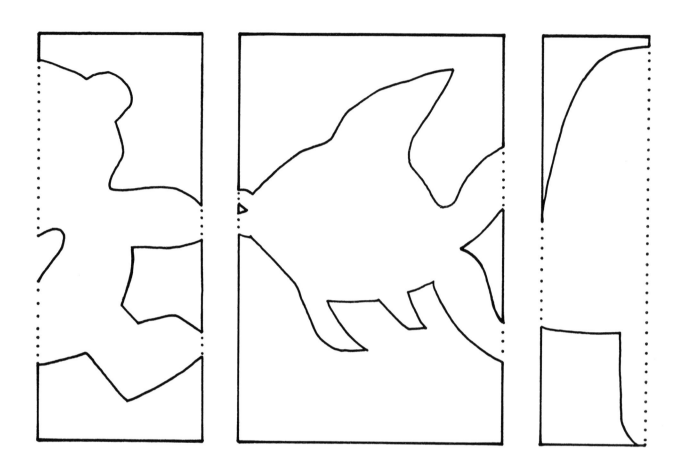

Accordion-fold paper strips to match the size of the pattern.
Tape or trace pattern onto paper and cut.
Be sure the dotted lines touch the edges.

POPSICLE® PEOPLE

Finish the faces for the Popsicle® People.
Cut them out and tell a story about them.

HIP, HIP, HOORAY
HAPPY SUMMER DAY.
HIP, HIP, HOORAY
A PARADE IS ON THE WAY.

Costume Party Parade

Designate one day as "Costume Party Parade Day." Have children bring old clothes from home to portray a character they would like to be — a television star, a clown, a king or queen, a child from another country, a storybook character, or even a teacher or principal. Or create costumes from paper sacks (page 37). Stage the parade early in the day so children will have the rest of the day to wear and enjoy the costumes. Invite two or three fun-loving adults to serve as judges. Award prizes for the "Most Original," the "Best Character Portrayal," and the "Funniest Costume." Be sure to explain the "rules" for winning a prize before the parade. Use the award patterns (pages 35 and 56) to cut winners' badges from construction paper, foil, or gift wrap.

PARADES II

Proud To Be Me Parade

Help each child make a name pennant (page 55) and a coat of arms badge (page 57) to represent his/her ethnic background, family history, or other symbol of cultural importance to the child. Plan for the parade to take place in the gym or on the playground where there will be plenty of room for stamping, stomping, swinging, and swaying to the music.

We Love Books Parade

Have each student proudly present a favorite book by holding it high as the book parade winds its way before another class or through the halls. Be sure to provide an immediate follow-up time for showing and discussing the books. For added excitement you could use the bookmark pattern (page 56) to make parade favors for the occasion.

PARADES III

Hat Parade

Plan one day to be "Hat Parade Day." Have children bring old or favorite hats from home to portray a character they would like to be – a television star, a baseball player, a cowboy or cowgirl, a child from another country, a storybook character, or even a teacher or principal. Stage the parade early in the day so children will have the rest of the day to wear and enjoy the hats. Invite two or three fun-loving adults to serve as judges. Award prizes for the "Most Original," the "Best Character Portrayal," and the "Funniest Hat." Be sure to explain the "rules" for winning a prize before the parade. Use the award patterns (pages 35 and 56) to cut winners' badges from construction paper, foil, or gift wrap.

Flag Parade

Help students make flags (page 55) to color, cut out, and attach to tree limbs or dowel sticks to wave proudly as the parade marches in single file with pomp and circumstance to patriotic music.

PENNANT PATTERN

AWARD BADGES

EXHiBiTOR
SUMMER
SCIENCE
FAIR

© 1991 by Incentive Publications, Inc., Nashville, TN.

Science
Fair
Award

© 1991 by Incentive Publications, Inc., Nashville, TN.

READING IS COOL!

SUN OIL

© 1991 by Incentive Publications, Inc., Nashville, TN.

1 ST

© 1991 by Incentive Publications,
Inc., Nashville, TN.

COAT OF ARMS PATTERN

Color, cut out, and add your own symbols to make a family coat of arms

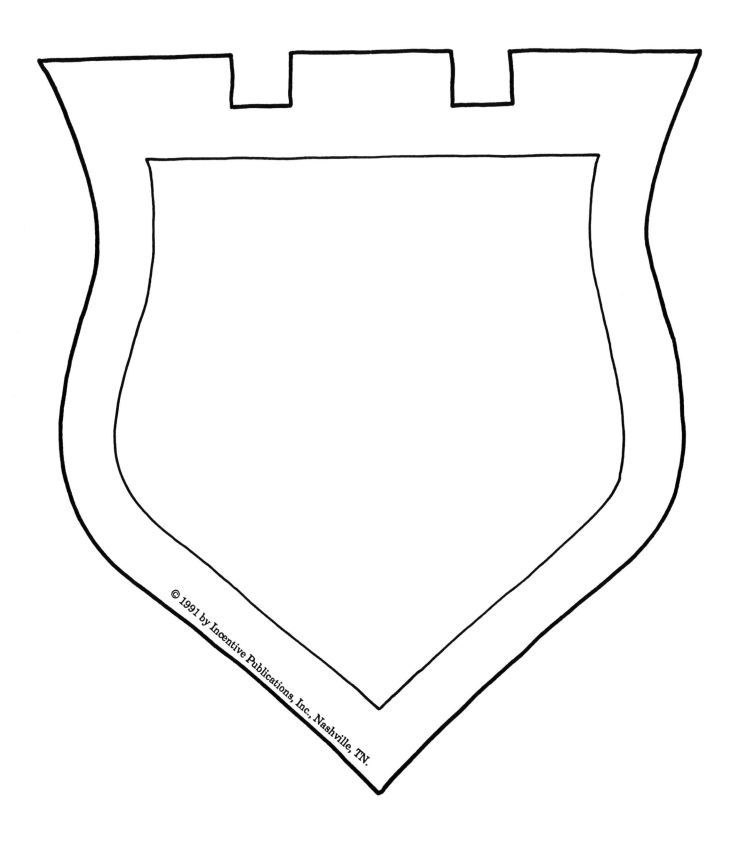

© 1991 by Incentive Publications, Inc., Nashville, TN.

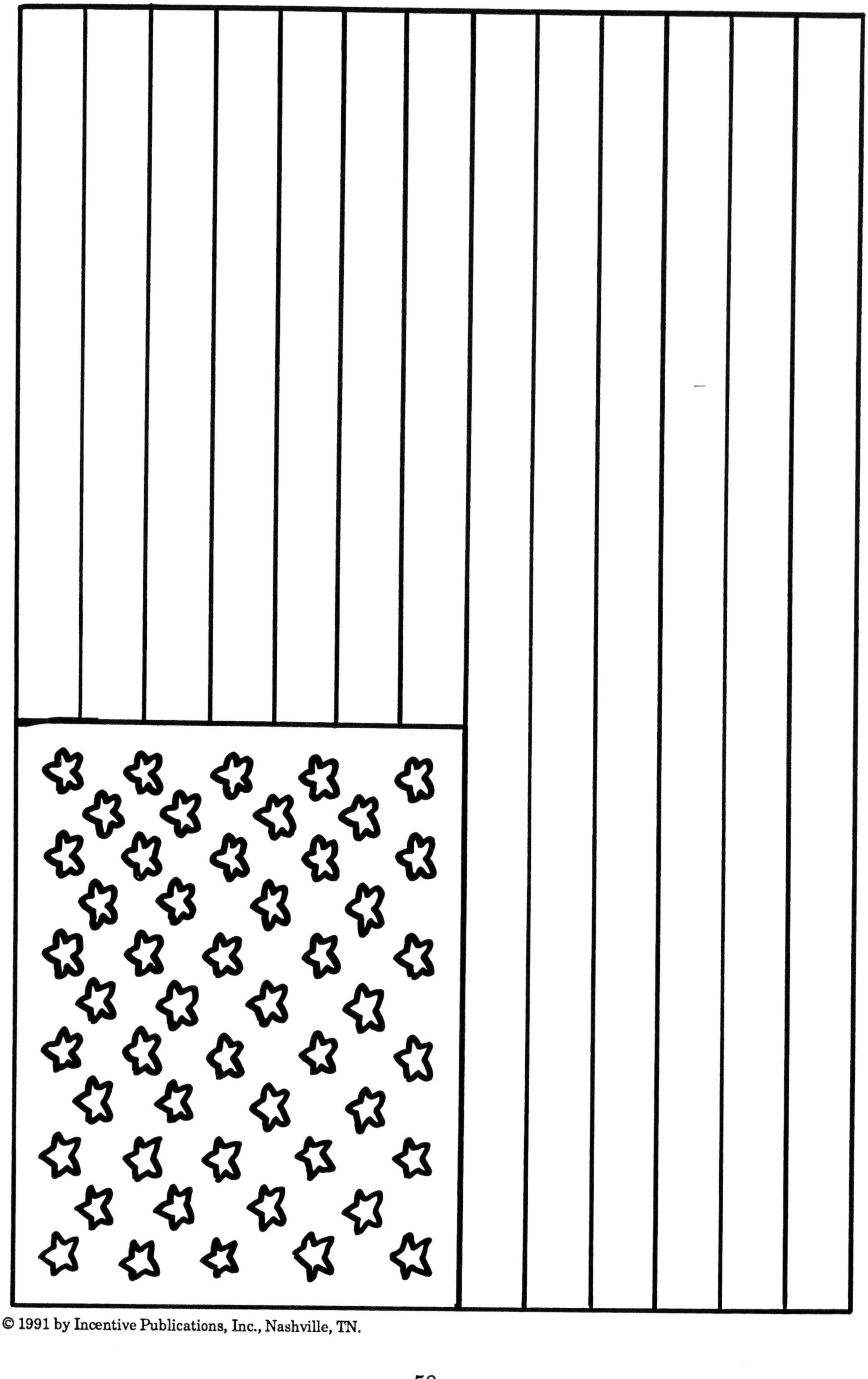

PLEDGE OF ALLEGIANCE TO THE FLAG

I pledge allegiance to the flag
of the United States of America,
and to the republic
for which it stands,
one nation, under God,
indivisible,
with liberty and justice
for all.

JULY DOORKNOB DECORATION

Color and cut out this doorknob decoration.
Hang it on you door to say that it's party day!

TEN TERRIFIC THINGS
TO DO IN AUGUST

1. **Have a tea party.** Make sun tea and serve it in pretty paper cups. First, use a big glass jar with a tight-fitting lid. Place some herb tea bags in the bottom of the jar and fill the jar with cold water. Leave the jar in a sunny spot for about four hours. Serve your tea with lemon and honey. It's fun to make and even more fun to drink.

2. **Enjoy a little bit of A-Lotta-Chocolate No-Bake Cookies.** (These cookies are very rich so a little bit goes a long way.) Here's how... In a large mixing bowl, combine an 8oz. jar of marshmallow creme, 1/2 cup of chocolate syrup, 6 cups of a puffed rice cereal (add more if the cookies are too sticky.), 1/2 cup chopped nuts (optional), and 1/2 cup flaked coconut (optional). Stir until all ingredients are well-mixed. Drop by teaspoonsful onto waxed paper. Enjoy!

3. **Prepare a Popsicle® party.** Buy a variety of flavored Popsicles® to enjoy outside. Sing songs, tell stories, and nevermind the drip, drip, drip! After all, it's super summertime!

4. **Plan a brown bag picnic.** Have students bring a sandwich and fruit from home. You furnish drinks and old-fashioned games. "Play Hide and Seek"; "I Spy"; "Mother, May I?"; relay races; "Red Light, Green Light"; and "Farmer Takes A Wife."

TEN TERRIFIC THINGS TO DO...

5. Stage a super summer science fair. Help children plan and carry out simple, short-term science projects that relate to the summer season. Observation journals, plant propagation, pollution, insect habits, and rock and fossil collections would make good topics. Use the award patterns (pages 35 and 56). Make sure every child receives an entry award.

6. Take a nature walk. Look for signs of summer and discuss birds, bees, trees, flowers, insects, etc., in their summer state as opposed to their winter, spring, and fall appearances.

7. Make nature collages. Collect twigs, leaves, small stones, etc., to use in collages. Back in the classroom, help children arrange the found objects on various sizes and colors of construction paper.

8. Print a painting. You will need little feet or hands, large sheets of white drawing paper, a big pan, a pot of tempera paint, lots of wet paper towels, a sense of humor, and plenty of patience. Mix water with the paint until the paint is relatively thin. (Test the consistency by dipping your hand in it and making a trial print.) Spread the sheets of drawing paper on a hard surface. One at a time, allow children to dip their hand or foot into the paint pan then place it

TEN TERRIFIC THINGS TO DO...

flat on the paper to make a print. (Clean feet and hands with warm water and paper towels.) When the hand or footprint dries, simple elements may be added with crayons, markers, and other materials (cotton balls, glitter, yarn, etc.) to turn the prints into imaginary animals, flowers, trees, birds, bees, etc. With careful planning, this project will not be as messy as it sounds, and the finished prints are quite spectacular.

9. **Get to know your community.** Summer is a marvelous time to visit the local fire hall, police station, or museum. Other places to visit include the public library, post office, city hall, or bank. If possible, arrange to use public transportation. A ride on the trolley or city bus makes these outings memorable as well as educational.

10. **Put on a play and invite another class to come.** Use a fairy tale such as *Chicken Licken* or *Hanzel and Gretel* as the basis of the play. Simply tell the story to the children, help them choose parts, and improvise the script. Practice a few times, adding simple props and costumes (scores, crepe paper hats, streamers, extra large T-shirts, etc.) Or, help the children make finger puppets to use with the stories. Patterns on page 69 will help you get started.

FIVE LITTLE FISH
SWIMMING IN THE SEA

(A finger play)

Five little fish swimming in the sea,
The first fish said,"That fisherman won't catch me!"
The second fish said, "Look out for that line!"
The third fish said, "That hook is not mine."
The fourth fish said, "We'd better swim away."
The fifth fish said, "We'll swim here another day."

So as fast as they could,
Like little fish should;
Away from the hook,
Without a backward look;
Five little fish swam out to sea,
Away from the fisherman, away from me!

FIVE LITTLE FISH FINGER PUPPETS

Color and cut out the finger puppets.
Tape the puppets together and act out the poem.

Name _____

A FUNNY CATCH

Follow the numbers, 1 to 23.
And a funny, funny catch you will see.

Following directions/numeral recognition

© 1991 by Incentive Publications, Inc., Nashville, TN.

CHICKEN LICKEN
(A summer day story to tell or act out)

One hot summer day, an acorn fell from a tree and hit Chicken Licken on the head.

"Cluck! Cluck! The sky is falling!" cried Chicken Licken excitedly. "I must warn the King."

As she hurried down the road to the King's palace, she met Cocky Locky who asked where she was going. "I'm going to tell the King that the sky is falling!" clucked Chicken Licken.

"Cock-a-doodle-doo!" crowed Cocky Locky. "I must come, too!"

As Chicken Licken and Cocky Locky walked along the road to the King's palace, they met Ducky Lucky who wanted to know where they were going in such a hurry.

We're on our way to tell the King that the sky is falling," said Chicken Licken and Cocky Locky.

"Quack! Quack! That sounds like something a duck should help do," said Ducky Lucky. "I'll come with you."

Chicken Licken, Cocky Locky, and Ducky Lucky clucked, crowed, and quacked on their way to the King's palace. They soon met Goosey Loosy who curiously asked where they were headed.

"We are on our way to tell the King that the sky is falling," answered the three.

"Honk! Honk! What you need is a goose in the group," said Goosey Loosy. "I'll join your troop."

So, Chicken Licken, Cocky Locky, Ducky Lucky, and Goosey Loosy clucked, crowed, quacked, and honked as they marched on to the King's palace.

Turkey Lurkey strutted around a bend in the road to ask where this noisy crew was going.

"To the palace, of course, to tell the King that the sky is falling," the group replied.

"Gobble! Gobble! I'm with you as quick as a flash!" said Turkey Lurkey with a dash.

Chicken Licken, Cocky Locky, Ducky Lucky, Goosey Loosy, and Turkey Lurkey clucked, crowed, quacked, honked, and gobbled more loudly than ever. They never noticed Foxy Loxy lurking beside the road.

"Ah, ho! What is such a handsome crew up to?" asked Foxy Loxy.

The proud animals answered, "Cluck! Cluck! Cock-a-doodle-doo! Quack! Quack! Honk! Honk! Gobble! Gobble! Haven't you heard? The sky is falling! The sky is falling! We are on our way to tell the King."

"Since I know the King well, perhaps I could be your guide," said Foxy Loxy.

"Please! Please! Do point the way since we must arrive today!" answered the self-appointed messengers.

So, Foxy Loxy, who actually intended to trap himself a fine dinner, led the barnyard crew to the deep, dark hole that served as his den. Just then a mighty roar came from within and Brian Lion stuck out his head searching for a tasty snack.

Chicken Licken stopped short of Foxy Loxy's black hole and clucked, "Run friends, run fast, for one step more could be your last!"

People from miles around heard the "Cluck! Cluck! Cock-a-doodle-doo! Quack! Quack! Honk! honk! Gobble! Gobble!" as the frightened animals fled back to the barnyard. The King was never told that the sky was falling.

CHICKEN LICKEN
FINGER PUPPETS

Color and cut out the finger puppets.
Tape the puppets together and act out the story.

· Chicken Licken ·

· Ducky Lucky ·

· Cocky Locky ·

· Goosey Loosy ·

· Turkey Lurkey ·

· Foxy Loxy ·

· Brian Lion ·

Name _____

SHAPES TO PASTE

Cut and paste the shapes at the bottom of the page in place to find a summer delight.

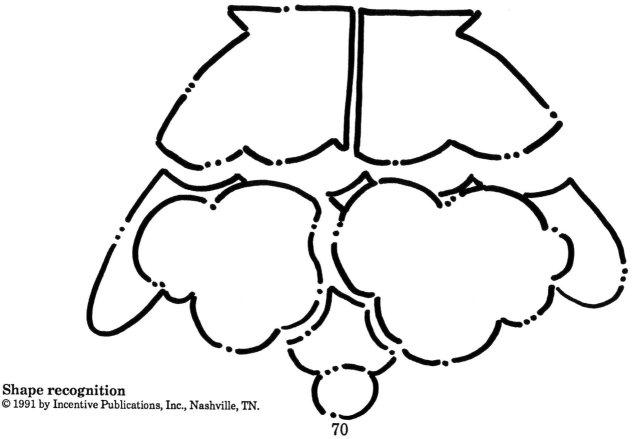

SUPER SUMMER SAFETY RULES

☆ I will never wander from the group when I am playing outside.

☆ I will never throw a ball toward windows or anyone who is not looking.

☆ I will always wear shoes when I am playing outside.

☆ I will never put wild berries, leaves, nuts, or objects from the ground into my mouth.

☆ I will always point sharp objects down, and I will never run with them.

☆ I will never play with or place plastic bags over my head.

☆ I will never pick up, play with, or catch plants, insects, or animals that I do not know.

NAME: _____

FRESH AIR, SUNSHINE, AND EXERCISE ARE GOOD FOR YOU

Swim

Walk

Swing

Hop

Skip

Jump

Breathe Deeply

Climb

Stretch

FLOWER POWER

Find the flower hidden in the picture.
Color the spaces marked "Y" yellow.
Color the spaces marked "G" green.
Color the spaces marked "B" blue.

Following directions/visual discrimination
© 1991 by Incentive Publications, Inc., Nashville, TN.

A SUMMER GARDEN

Color 4 vegetables green in the picture.
Color 2 fruits red in the picture.
Tell a story about what will happen next in the garden.

Following directions/visual discrimination
© 1991 by Incentive Publications, Inc., Nashville, TN.

SUMMER DAY RHYMES
TO ACT OUT

Jack and Jill
Went up the hill
To fetch a pail of water.
Jack fell down
And broke his crown
And Jill came tumbling after.

Little Miss Muffet
Sat on a tuffet
Eating her curds and whey.
Along came a spider
Who sat down beside her
And frightened Miss Muffet
away!

Little Boy Blue,
Come blow your horn,
The sheep's in the meadow,
The cow's in the corn.

Where is the boy
Who looks after the sheep?
He's under the haystack
Fast asleep.

Will you wake him?
No, not I!
For if I do,
He's sure to cry.

Name _____

FUN IN THE SUN

Find and color all the letters of the alphabet hiding in this picture.

Letter recognition

AUGUST DOORKNOB DECORATION

Color and cut out the doorknob decoration.
Hang it on your door to say that you are outside enjoying the good old summertime.

BIBLIOGRAPHY

Are You My Friend? Gyo Fujikawa, Random House.
Playing, talking, sharing and exploring are beautifully portrayed as some of the pleasures shared by special friends as they have been learning and growing together.

Around The Year. Tasha Tudor, Henry Z. Walck, Inc.
Summer pleasures are celebrated through beautiful childlike illustrations in context with the other three seasons.

Best Friends. Steven Kellog, Dial Books for Young Readers.
Two best friends are separated when one of the friends goes to visit relatives for the summer and the friend left behind copes with loneliness and new emotions.

Birdsong Lullaby. Diane Stanley, William Morrow and Company.
A little girl and her mother share a beautiful bedtime lullaby that allows them to imagine the thrill of soaring through the air, light as a feather and free as a bird.

Games. Imogene Forte, Incentive Publications.
Games, old and new, requiring little preparation and using materials readily available in classrooms and homes, provides both inside and outside pleasure and fun with an added learning bonus.

The Girl Who Would Rather Climb Trees. Miriam Schlein, Harcourt Brace Javonovich.
Melissa loves to bird watch, roller skate, cook, work puzzles, read and lots of other things, but most of all she loves to climb trees.

Mrs. Minetta's Car Pool. Elizabeth Spurr, Macmillan.
Mrs. Minetta's magic car pool transports the children to four marvelous destinations allowing them to experience adventures at the beach, in snowy hills, inside an amusement park and at a dude ranch.

My First Nature Book. Angela Wilkes, Alfred A. Knopf.
Indoor and outdoor activities such as, collecting, planting and watching seeds grow, making a bottle garden, tracking pets, and keeping a nature diary encourage observation and appreciation of nature.

One Morning In Maine. Robert McCloskey, Viking Press.
A little girl named Sal enjoys a beautiful day at the beach while experiencing "growing pains" associated with the loss of a tooth.

One Summer Night. Eleanor Schick, Green Willow Books.
When a little girl named Laura decides to dance instead of going to bed on a warm summer night, all sorts of unusual events begin to take place in the urban neighborhood in which she lives.

The Relatives Came. Cynthia Rylant, Bradberry Press.
When relatives come for a visit, fun, games, food, hugs, laughter, and music fill the house. The story begins with the visitors' arrival, progresses through joyous sharing, and ends with their departure amid plans for next summer.

Sea Swan. Kathryn Lasky, Macmillan.
A great "read aloud" story, about a grandmother in Boston who decides to learn to swim on the morning of her 75th birthday and sets in motion a whole string of wonderful events.

The Socksnatchers. Lorna Balian, Abingdon Press.
The socksnatchers who live in the cellar of the Perkins' family home continue their sock snatching undetected until the family cat intervenes.

Summer Story. Maxine W. Kumin, G.P. Putnam's Sons.
A see and read story book in verse that delightfully captures the essence and joy of summer days.

Tomie De Paola's Mother Goose. Tomie de Paola, G.P. Putnam's Sons.
A fancifully illustrated collection of over 200 Mother Goose nursery rhymes to supplement and enrich a wide variety of summer projects.

INDEX